A Note to Parents

For many children, learning math!" is their first response — add "Me, too!" Children often see adults comfortably reading and writing, but they rarely have such models for mathematics. And math fear can be catching!

The easy-to-read stories in this **Hello Math Reader!** series were written to give children a positive introduction to mathematics and parents a pleasurable reacquaintance with a subject that is important in everyone's life. **Hello Math Reader!** stories make mathematical ideas accessible, interesting, and fun for children. The activities and suggestions at the end of each book provide parents with a hands-on approach to help children develop mathematical interest and confidence.

Enjoy the mathematics!
• Give your child a chance to retell the story. The more familiar children are with the story, the more they will understand its mathematical concepts.
• Use the colorful illustrations to help children "hear and see" the math at work in the story.
• Treat the math activities as games to be played for fun. Follow your child's lead. Spend time on those activities that engage your child's interest and curiosity.
• Activities, especially ones using physical materials, help make abstract mathematical ideas concrete.

Learning is a messy process and learning about math calls for children to become immersed in lively experiences that help them make sense of mathematical concepts and symbols.

Although learning about numbers is basic to math, other ideas, such as identifying shapes and patterns, measuring, collecting and interpreting data, reasoning logically, and thinking about chance are also important. By reading these stories and having fun with the activities, you will help your child enthusiastically say "**Hello, math**," instead of "I hate math."

—Marilyn Burns
National Mathematics Educator
Author of *The I Hate Mathematics! Book*

God bless America and all of her children.
— *C.N.*

With appreciation and gratitude to Edie Weinberg, a real Art Director Champ, and to my 2002 Grad Champs, Zart and Christel
— *C.O.*

No part of this publication may be reproduced in whole or in part, or stored in a retrieval system, or transmitted in any form or by any means, electronic, mechanical, photocopying, recording, or otherwise, without written permission of the publisher. For information regarding permission, write to Scholastic Inc., Attention: Permissions Dept., 557 Broadway, New York, NY 10012.

Copyright © 2002 by Scholastic Inc.
The activities on pages 27-32 copyright © 2000 by Marilyn Burns
All rights reserved. Published by Scholastic Inc.

SCHOLASTIC, HELLO MATH READER! are trademarks
and/or registered trademarks of Scholastic Inc.

ISBN 0-439-24230-4

12 11 10 9 8 7 6 5 4 3 2   2 3 4 5 6 7/0

Printed in the U.S.A. • First printing, November 2002

The Chocolate Champs

By Cindy Neuschwander
Illustrated by Cristina Ong

Hello Math Reader! — Level 3

SCHOLASTIC INC.
New York   Toronto   London   Auckland   Sydney
Mexico City   New Delhi   Hong Kong   Buenos Aires

"Yum!" said Eric. "Candy bars!"

"They look good!" said Maylee.

"Please listen, everyone," said Ms. Wang. "Our class is having a one-day candy-bar sales contest! We'll use the money for a field trip to the zoo. Our top seller will earn a special prize. The Chocolate Champ will win a ride on the zoo elephant!"

"Woo-hoo!" the class cheered.

"Hunky Chunks cost $1.25 each," said Ms. Wang. "Little Nibbles cost 50 cents each. Make tally marks for the candy you sell. Collect the money. Then pass out the candy."

After school, the whole class rushed home to sell candy bars.

Eric had no luck. Everyone on his street had bought cookies at a bake sale at city hall. "I'm on a diet now," said one neighbor.

Maylee's family had just ordered popcorn from her older sister's class sale. "It's your turn next time," said Maylee's mom. "I already spent my allowance," said her brother.

The next morning, Maylee met Eric on the way to school. "I didn't sell any candy," she said.

"Me, either," Eric replied.

"Hey!" said Maylee. "Maybe we can sell some candy here at school!"

"Great idea!" said Eric.

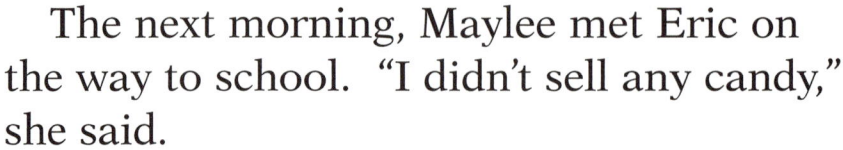

The two kids hurried to the lunchroom. They saw Mrs. Holly, the school cook.

"Hello!" said Mrs. Holly. "You're a bit early for lunch."

"Would you like to buy some candy?" asked Eric. "We're earning money for a trip to the zoo."

"I LOVE candy!" said Mrs. Holly. "I'll buy two Hunky Chunks. I'll also take two Little Nibbles." Eric made four tally marks.

Maylee started adding. "Two Hunky Chunks? $2.50. Two Little Nibbles? $1.00. That will be $3.50, please."

Mrs. Holly handed Maylee three dollar bills and two quarters.

"Our first sale!" cheered Eric. "Look out! Here come the Chocolate Champs."

"Come on! Let's sell some more," said Maylee.

Eric and Maylee hurried around the school.
"KNOCK, KNOCK." They tapped on Mr. Garrott's door. Mr. Garrott fixed things at school. He opened the tool room door.
Mr. Garrott had a parrot named Bud.
"Hello!" said Mr. Garrott.
"HELLO!" said Bud.
"Will you buy some candy?" asked Maylee.

"Oh, yes!" said Mr. Garrott.
"OH, YES!" said Bud.
"I'll buy 6 Hunky Chunks," said Mr. Garrott.

"SQUAWK!" said Bud.

"And one Little Nibble for Bud," said Mr. Garrott. Bud clicked his beak.

Eric made 7 tally marks. He and Maylee patted Bud. Then they hurried off.

They visited Ms. Flutter in the music room.
"Come in! Come in!" sang Ms. Flutter.

"Ms. Flutter, will you buy some candy? It will help send our class to the zoo," said Maylee.

"Yes, yes, yes!" sang Ms. Flutter. "Singing makes me hungry. I'll buy one Little Nibble."

"50 cents, please," said Eric. He made one tally mark.

"Oh, oh, oh!" sang Ms. Flutter. "I only have one dollar."

"We can give you change," said Maylee. "One dollar minus 50 cents is 50 cents in change."

"We're the Chocolate Champs!" said Eric.

"Not yet," said Maylee. "We need to sell more!"

"Ooops!" said Eric. "We forgot to get our money from Mr. Garrott."

"Let's go!" said Maylee.

Mr. Garrott was way across the playground.

"Let's cut through the field," said Eric. They ran into the soccer team. The team was practicing.

TWEET! The coach's whistle blew. Practice was over.

"Want to buy some candy?" Eric and Maylee asked.

"Sure!" said 10 soccer players.

"Me, too!" said the goalie. "I'll take one," said the coach.

They all wanted Hunky Chunks. Eric made 12 tally marks.

"That's $15.00!" counted Maylee. "Now we need to see Mr. Garrott."

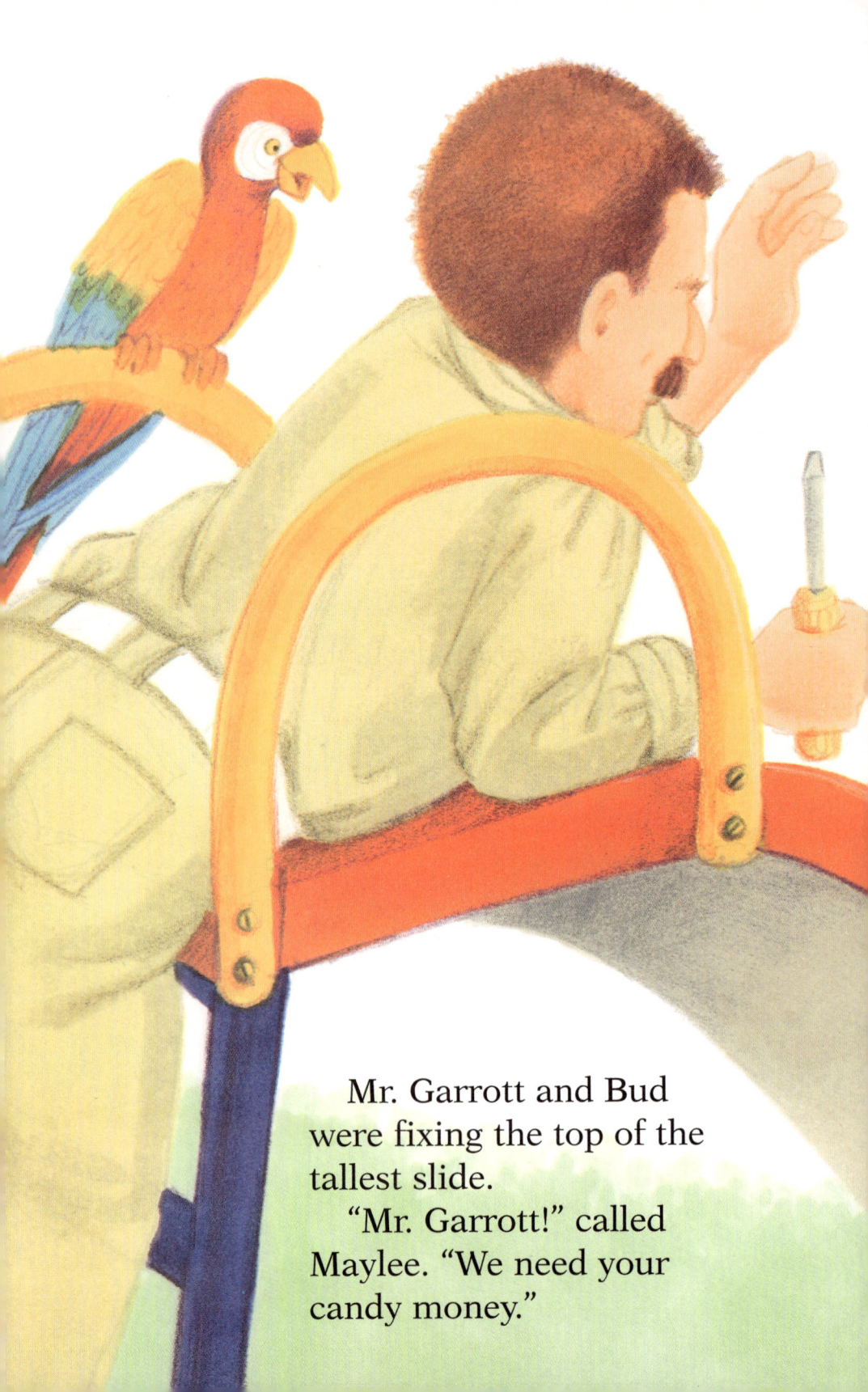

Mr. Garrott and Bud were fixing the top of the tallest slide.

"Mr. Garrott!" called Maylee. "We need your candy money."

"Coming!" yelled Mr. Garrott.

WHOOSH! Mr. Garrott slid down the slide. WHOOSH! Bud flew down.

"HELLO!" said Bud.

"How much do I owe you?" asked Mr. Garrott.

Eric looked at his tally sheet. "You bought 6 Hunky Chunks and 1 Little Nibble," he said. "That's $8.00."

"I only have $10.00," said Mr. Garrott. "OH, YES!" said Bud.

"We can give you change," said Maylee. She counted out 2 dollars in quarters.

"Thank you!" said Mr. Garrott and his parrot.

Eric counted the tally marks.
"We've sold 24 candy bars," he said.
"Why stop now?" asked Maylee.
"We're on a roll."
VROOM! They saw Mr. Carr.
Mr. Carr drove the school bus.
"Mr. Carr!" yelled Eric. "Will you buy some candy? We have two kinds."
Mr. Carr leaned out the school bus window. He handed Eric $5.00. He said something and then drove away.

"I didn't hear what Mr. Carr ordered," said Eric.

"We can figure it out," said Maylee. "It adds up to $5.00."

"Ten Little Nibbles cost $5.00," said Eric.

"So do four Hunky Chunks," said Maylee. "Two Hunky Chunks and five Little Nibbles also cost $5.00."

"Let's have all three kinds ready. We'll give Mr. Carr the right ones when he comes back," said Eric.

Soon Mr. Carr drove back. "I'll take those Little Nibbles now," he said. Eric and Maylee handed him the candy. The school bell rang.

Eric wrote both their names on the tally sheet. Then he and Maylee headed into class.

Ms. Wang collected all the tally sheets. "Well," she said. "Looks like we'll definitely be going to the zoo! Everyone sold lots of candy! And the Chocolate Champ is..."

Eric and Maylee looked at each other. Eric crossed his fingers. Maylee gave him a "thumbs-up sign."

"Or should I say, the Chocolate Champs are...

"...Eric and Maylee! You've sold 34 candy bars and collected $32.00. Congratulations!"

Eric and Maylee walked to the front of the class and stood side by side. Ms. Wang handed them each a certificate for the elephant ride. The class clapped.

• About the Activities •

Learning about money is a basic, real-world skill. Children need to know the names of coins, how much each is worth, how to figure out the value of collections of coins, and how to relate coins and bills. *The Chocolate Champs* focuses specifically on quarters and bills, so all of the activities that follow on these pages give children practice in figuring with quarters and learning how quarters relate to larger amounts of money.

The quarter is a unique coin in that its name relates to its value. There's no such connection for our other coins — the names penny, nickel, and dime have nothing to do with the values of $.01, $.05, or $.10! Children simply have to learn the names of these coins and their values, and they do so from their many experiences using them in the real world. In the same way, they first learn the name and value of a quarter. Later, however, children make the connection that since four quarters equal $1.00, it makes mathematical sense that a coin worth $.25 is called a quarter. Children also eventually connect one-fourth of a dollar with the words "quarter dollar" that appear on the front of the coin. Focusing on quarters not only builds children's understanding of money, it supports their number sense and also lays a foundation for their later study of fractions and decimals.

Keep in mind that the best way for children to learn about money is to give them many firsthand opportunities to use money in real-world and play situations. Be open to your child's interests and have fun with these activities!

—Marilyn Burns

> You'll find tips and suggestions for guiding the activities whenever you see a box like this!

Retelling the Story

Hunky Chunks cost $1.25 each. Little Nibbles cost $ .50 each.

Eric and Maylee made their first candy sale to Mrs. Holly. She bought two of each kind. Maylee figured out that Mrs. Holly owed $3.50. How did Maylee figure?

Mr. Garrott bought six Hunky Chunks for himself and one Little Nibble for his parrot, Bud. Eric and Maylee gave Mr. Garrott the candy but forgot to collect the money. How much did Mr. Garrott owe for the candy?

> It may help to give your child a collection of quarters and dollar bills to use to figure out these problems. It's fine to make paper dollar bills and cut them out.

Ms. Flutter in the music room bought one Little Nibble, but she only had a $1.00 bill. How much change did she get? How did you figure?

How many candy bars did Mrs. Holly, Mr. Garrott, and Ms. Flutter buy all together?

Then the kids sold 12 Hunky Chunks to the soccer team and coach. Maylee figured out that those candy bars cost $15.00 all together. Was Maylee right? How do you know?

Next they went to collect the $8.00 from Mr. Garrott. Mr. Garrott had a $10.00 bill, so Maylee gave him $2.00 in change. She gave him all quarters. How many quarters did Maylee give Mr. Garrott?

They collected $3.50 from Mrs. Holly, $8.00 from Mr. Garrott, $ .50 from Ms. Flutter, and $15.00 from the soccer team. How much money did they collect so far?

Eric figured out that they had sold 24 candy bars so far. How many of these were Hunky Chunks and how many were Little Nibbles?

Next Eric and Maylee sold $5.00 worth of candy to Mr. Carr, but they didn't hear what he ordered. They figured out that he ordered either:

10 Little Nibbles or

4 Hunky Chunks or

2 Hunky Chunks and 5 Little Nibbles

Check that each of these possibilities costs $5.00. What did Mr. Carr really want?

Before Mr. Carr bought candy, Eric and Maylee had sold 24 candy bars. Now how many candy bars had they sold? Before Mr. Carr bought candy, Eric and Maylee had collected $27.00. When Mr. Carr paid $5.00, how much money did they have?

What did Maylee and Eric win for selling the most candy?

25
50
75
100
125
150
175
200
225
250
275
300
325
350
375
400
425
450

Counting Quarters

A quarter is worth 25 cents. Four quarters are worth 100 cents, which is the same as $1.00.

Can you count by 25s? Try it. Use the list of numbers to the left for help.

What patterns do you notice in the numbers that count by 25s?

Money Riddles

For all of these riddles, remember that one quarter is worth 25 cents.

I have two quarters. How much money do I have?

Mom gave me a $1.00 bill and one quarter. How much money did she give me?

I have three quarters. How much money do I have?

I had four quarters, but I gave one to my sister. How much money do I have?

I had a $1.00 bill and bought a drink for fifty cents. How many quarters did I get for change?

My grandpa gave me a handful of nine quarters! How much money did he give me?

I took a $5.00 bill to the bank and exchanged it for quarters. How many quarters did I get?

Race for $10.00

This is a game for two people. To play, you need 10 real quarters, 20 $1.00 bills, one $10.00 bill, and one die. (If you had 10 quarters, 20 $1.00 bills, and one $10.00 bill, how much money would you have? This is a lot of money, so make cutout play bills for the game.)

To Play

Put all the money in piles of quarters and bills. When it's your turn, roll the die. The number that comes up tells you how many quarters to take. If you have four quarters, exchange them for a $1.00 bill. When you're finished with your turn, pass the die to the other player.

The winner is the first player to exchange 10 $1.00 bills for a $10.00 bill.

Chocolate Price Sheet

It may have helped Eric and Maylee to figure out how much different numbers of candy bars cost before they started their candy sale. Can you help them fill in this chart?

Little Nibbles		Hunky Chunks	
1	$ .50	1	$ 1.25
2	$ 1.00	2	$ 2.50
3	$ 1.50	3	
4	$ 2.00	4	$ 5.00
5		5	
6		6	
7	$ 3.50	7	$ 8.75
8		8	
9		9	$11.25
10	$ 5.00	10	$12.50

The $10.00 Challenge

If you had $10.00 to spend, you could buy all Hunky Chunks, all Little Nibbles, or some of each. Figure out what you could buy so that you didn't have any change left over.

> It's not necessary for children to figure all the possible ways to spend exactly $10.00 on Hunky Chunks and Little Nibbles. Let children work on the problem as long as they are interested.